D0843374

Shimming the Glass House

Poems by

Helen Pruitt Wallace

The Ashland Poetry Press
Ashland University
Ashland, Ohio 44805

Printed in the United States of America

ISBN: 978-0-912592-63-3

LCCN#: 2008931672

Book cover design by Mike Ruhe

Cover art: "The Patient Gardener" by Maggie Taylor

Author photo by Lisa Munafo, D&L Photography

Thank you to the editors of the following journals in which these poems, some in earlier versions, first appeared:

Clockwatch Review, "The Surgeon As Patient"
Cumberland Poetry Review, "Sixth Grade Science Fair"
Kalliope, "Refusing to Set Back the Clock"
Nimrod: An International Journal, "After Auden's *Musée des Beaux Arts,*" "Cracks of Light," "Confession to the Muse," and "Renovating an Old House After the World Changed"
Penumbra, "Trappings"
Sundog: The Southeast Review, "A Predatory Songbird Without Talons"
The Florida Humanities, "In Praise of the Beehive"
The Literary Review: An International Quarterly, "Between Cracks"
The Lyric, "When We Least Expect It"
The MacGuffin, "Dapping On Black Lake" and "A Predatory Songbird Without Talons" (reprint)
The Midwest Quarterly, "Black Dirt"
Tampa Review, "Studying Your Hands" and "Jane Deals with Infidelity"

"A Mother Considers a Cloned World" appeared in the anthology *Divided Again: Poems About Designing People.* Thanks to the Edmonds Institute for awarding this poem first place in their 1999 contest.

Thanks to the Academy of American Poets for selecting "Gator on Lake Ashby" for a McKay Shaw Poetry Award, and to the dA Center for the Arts and Deborah Bogen for awarding "Epilogues for a Brother" first place in their 2007 contest.

I am grateful to the following friends and teachers for their many artistic insights: Peter Meinke, Enid Shomer, Sheila Ortiz-Taylor, Janet Burroway, David Kirby, Hunt Hawkins, Van Brock, Lisa Birnbaum, Silvia Curbello, Kim Garcia, Donna Long, Donald Morrill, Elaine Smith, Wendy Buffington, and especially to Peter Wallace for his generous heart, constant support, and keen eye. Thanks, too, to the Virginia Center for the Creative Arts where several of these poems were written, and to The Sewanee Writers' Conference for supporting me with a Tennessee Williams' Scholarship. Lastly, thanks to Robert Phillips for selecting this manuscript for the Richard Snyder Prize, and to the good folks at Ashland Poetry Press — Stephen Haven, Deborah Fleming, and especially Sarah Wells for her gracious attention to my work.

For Peter, Daniel, and Hannah,
and for my parents, Frances and Crayton

Contents

III

I

. . . our house is open, there are no keys in the doors,
and invisible guests come in and out at will.
—Czeslaw Milosz

Conjuring Light

I was thinking about the Sistine Chapel:
how Michelangelo's Adam, called up by the fingertip
        of God, reminds us we're nothing
without touch. Unless you look again,

        a little closer. He's fully formed,
all sinuous and buff, with light glancing
        off his languid flesh, despite the hint
their fingers haven't met,

        the milky space left between their reach?
I, a daughter of Eve, might argue
        we're made from what we make,
which reminds me of the butter cow

        displayed at the Iowa State Fair:
600 pounds of lathed creamy flanks, belly,
        and hooves, with swirls of light smeared
across its haunches, a new-age fatted calf

        prepared for our prodigal world.
But then I think of us, and how
        sometimes in the blue haze of morning,
daubed by the resin of sleep,

        I'm not sure if the curve beneath
the sheet is yours or mine—
        or what to call the force we conjure there
that with one touch sends us hurling into dawn.

3

Between Cracks

I seek dilapidation,
dirt roads hidden in weeds
leading to bare-boned shacks.
I like the gray sag
of split boards, the stubborn lean,
the unhinged door, glass scattered
lightly on the floor, fallen
from a web of broken pane.

What's left behind
acquires a subtle grace,
a skewed particularity
caught in the glare
of time made visible with age:
a leather shoe, curled
and hard, a chipped plate,
a rusted bottle cap,

and just the smell
of staid abandonment, the dank
odor caught between cracks,
cracks themselves
splintered, warped,
gaping
at what might have been,
and open to anything at all.

Vietnamese Children Picking Kumquats

They run to our yard laughing,
       knapsacks slung across their backs

to shake loose kumquats
       from a tree. Two or three

jostle a limb, one prefers to jump
       and pluck. A beagle

circles them barking, as they stuff
       the fruit in pockets

beneath a dollop of sun. Their hair
       is the black of cormorants

fishing the surf, their words
       the surf itself, high-pitched,

splashing. I offer cartons of juice
       they take from me shyly

but it's they who offer me a rare
       abundance—some glimmer

of a light that drew them seaward,
       despite the many shapes terror took

when what was theirs
       was all that they could carry.

Epilogues for a Brother
for Mark Pruitt, 1960–1985

1. Rewriting the Last Flight

You do it like the hero in the movie: eject
just before the plumed crash, your white chute

floating like milkweed toward some grassy
field. And there, a girl, her black dog,

maybe tossing pebbles in a stream
or gathering fistfuls of daisies,

drops her wicker basket on the ground, and races
for the sun's pearled glare.

She finds you in a puddle of silk, dazed, bruised
barely but enough to need her soft shoulder

as you hobble to her house for soup
and the buoyant rest of your life.

2. Minghun Bride: Afterlife Marriage

Assume the rest of your life doesn't happen.
Take this burnt offering of cash,

and to cruise the netherworld, a paper model
of a Cessna SE. Like those along

the Yellow River Canyon seeking dead wives
for dead sons to bury them side by side,

I, too, would offer gold, 10,000 yuan: a dowry
for the dead, if you, brother, wanted a bride.

Who's to say desire won't outlive us?
In the Loess Plateau the poorest parents weave

the wives from straw, trusting the chemistry
of dirt. There's wisdom in a match like that.

After Auden's *Musée des Beaux Arts*

Auden's right about disaster, the way it often finds us
in the ordinary. I could duplicate the angle of the broom,
the pattern of renegade dirt evading the pan, the smell
of Pop Tarts burning in a toaster. Everyone you loved
was busy living—checking e-mail, cleaning gutters,
slicing red tomatoes on a plate. Our days stack one by one
upon such rituals, familiar acts that shim our fragile world
to something, if not balanced, almost holy.
So how were we to know your last breath, sent out
like a good dog to fetch, wouldn't come back?

Grief is too easily misperceived. Even now the void
you left could suck the churning sphere right down
with it, at least jam phonelines and traffic, unleash
a small monsoon, meteor. Perhaps it has. Catastrophes catapult
daily; who names the cause of chaos in the world?
Your mother folds and folds the white sheets
but see how her corners don't line up, and your father,
out raking leaves, notice his grip on the rake, how tightly he tries
to hold on, while the leaves, the leaves keep falling.
And over there, look, your black dog, crazed for a buried bone.

Studying Your Hands
for DL

Your day, you said,
      was good as any day,
till then. Then he coughed,
      loosened up his tie,
smoothed the hair
      that fell across your eyes,
and whispered,
      We should talk.

Outside you heard the kids,
      a neighbor's dog,
a car that stopped then started
      from a curb—
familiar sounds that kept
      your common world
knocking at that white block
      of time.

You watched a playful pattern
      on the wall
made of sun and lace,
      you traced a crack—
then studying your hands,
      your web of veins,
you felt creases smirking
      from your palm.

There comes a certain clarity
      with pain; the world
rewinding focuses again
      and shows the damnedest
things. You swore he'd never wear
      a paisley tie.
You swore you'd never have
      your mother's hands.

Renovating an Old House After the World Changed
September 12, 2001

I rise in the night to watch a tree stab the moon
over and over, light dripping through leaves.

The wind has found an unhooked door
to slap, and the plumbing makes no effort

to muffle its moan, as if the house itself predicts
our fall. Our endless renovations feel absurd

against this impending collapse. We drag
around our dread like a dirty blanket,

grief gripping our ankles. The walls of the house
are shaking. They lean toward something unknown.

What have we done to conjure such hatred—
whose blood on our own clenched fists?

By morning a pink horizon swells like a busted lip.
The moon still squints its severed eye.

10

Dapping on Black Lake

In that string of seconds when the stone defies natural law
we find a freedom which allows our minds to skip
across the water in brief defiance.
                                    —Audubon

For us I grip a gray, flat stone,
make a wish, fling it toward a lake,
one dark and open as a heart. Gravity craves

to be defied, like any law grown
leery of itself, the order of things
too unpredictable. I watch flint skip

across the pool, willing we could rid
the world of pain that sends dark rings

rippling out. A simple act of yearning—
skipping stones; with luck and flair
much can be surpassed. Like black ink

flicked across a page, the stone burns
a path—a blistering path—through deft air
that will not let it sink.

Carry a Stone on Your Tongue

to open the doors, windows, the absence
     to feel drenched in it
to hear the owl's note
     as the moon stuck in his beak

to feel the moon's implosion
     to burn with it
to know impetuous green
     beneath the damp dirt

to taste the damp dirt in the stone
     you place on your tongue
to quell thirst You hold it
     like an owl's note Like absence

12

Cardinal at the Bedroom Window

Red wing, black beak and eye, whirling, mad
   at the pane, whacking it over and over
as if to crack a life he never led,

or worry a wound that never bled—
   nor healed. Crazed as a thwarted lover,
red wing, black beak and eye, whirling, mad.

And in the room, a chair, table and bed,
   nothing to lure a bird, yet how he hovers
before this crack of light. A life never led

haunts us, like something inside bred
   of fear. What can we do when suffering—
that wing, beak and eye—whirls madly

around us? Listen to him knock. Should we,
   do we dare, let him in, or just cover
the crack of the life never led,

hoping he'll leave? Some wounds never bled
   though we worried them over and over.
Red wing, black beak and eye, whirling, mad.
   What happens to lives never led?

She Never Wears Anything but White

and floats through the city
like a sand dollar skeleton spit from surf
or a message in a vagrant corked jar
erased to a damp page.
Rifling through garbage cans
newspaper stuffed in her shoes,
she bears the bent grace of a gardener
intent on weeding impatiens,
chapped fingers delicately plucking.
And here, at this park where she lingers,
a noon sun softens its glare.
You wish you could offer her your lunch
but something in the tilt of her chin—
you leave it discreetly on a bench,
then notice as you pass her
a white gardenia tucked behind her ear,
beautiful and bruised.

Missed Calls
Madrid, March 11, 2004

Cell phones kept ringing from bodies of the dead,
      a cacophony of Bach and blues, as news
of horror spread: four trains exploding in Madrid.

Such a medley as the ground ran red,
      the dying—still so much to do—
listened to phones ringing, ringing from the dead,

as a chorus of ash kept building. Death led
      its own improvisation while panic grew
in the horror spreading in Madrid,

and beyond, as the world looked on. Black bags laid
      out like flat notes, each tolling a too
raw refrain: partial bodies of the dead

still toting their partial goods, a backpack filled
      with books, a purse, a baby's white shoe
intact in the horror of trains exploding in Madrid.

Dance, dance you dead ones! The morning's bled
      its light. Everyone you knew is calling you.
Listen—your cell phones are ringing. Who
will finally answer for the horror exploding in Madrid?

Absorbing Light

*What we see as color is the remains after
the material has absorbed its own private
and unique chime.*

——Philip Ball

This city with blaring graffiti and souped-up cars
in crowded parking lots, unrolls streets like bolts of gauze.
It offers up flowers in a park, the smell of fresh baguettes,
corner jazz, and sirens, ever sirens, to remind us
of the pitch of pain.
                I stroll these sidewalks the way
I move my hands across the pale back of my beloved,
looking for a warmth called *home* (we each relive a thousand
small evictions), and all around me hunger bares its teeth
in vacant stares and shuffled shopping carts, the gaping soles
of mismatched leather shoes.
                But look how the mystery of color
throbs sweetly from every neon sign—how matter absorbs
its chimes of light, deserts the rest. And beauty's born
in hues of this rejection; it pulses through the night in red, blue.
Does what we have make us who we are—or what we lose?

After Bishop's "One Art"

The art of losing isn't hard to master . . .
——Elizabeth Bishop

though hoarding's even easier to do.
The little things acquired over time
all become a subtle part of you.

Save something every day. Admit the true
significance of concert stubs, labels off fine
wine. Hoarding's so much easier to do

than craving what you carelessly threw
out: a napkin with a scribbled line
of verse that showed a vibrant part of you

lost along the way. Why master losing?
Who are we without minutiae to remind
us? Hoarding's even easier to do

with lavish goods: the fake jewels
too gaudy to wear, the pink china
stuck in a box . . . or envy . . . fear . . . parts of you

you quickly stash away. Oh, there are things you'd
gladly lose, like longing, that sad-eyed
bitch. She hoards your scent. She's part of you.
It's doubtful she'll ever leave your side.

Trappings

We're packing up the attic where boxes bulged ten years in mold and dust. They don't contain the gin they advertise. We wish they did. Instead they're full of books we never read, old hats, macramé belts, ceramic bowls we made in seventh grade, misshaped, fragile with pocks. They remind us of what we used to be, which may not be all bad, since even we are not our former selves. Each seven years all skin cells are replaced. Sloughed off with strands of dry hair, and toenails we trim and softly drop, or thoughts shoved through cortex, then lost in our graying bubble wrap. Our teeth, too, yellow, fall out. And sex, that hot commodity, we give with little more than bump and grind. So what's with all the obsolete loot we can't convince ourselves to leave behind? Like this—the box of wind-up toys that terrorized our cool, neurotic cat. Look, the monkey drumming with a stick, the alligator with the snapping jaw, that quirky dog that squats before each flip. Grab the lava lamps and clarinet, bottle rockets, peace signs and rugs. For now, despite what each of us was taught, it's better to take than give away. Our bodies may have mastered letting go, but even them we'll box some final day. Just in case. Besides, you never know.

Sestina Considering Mania
Garden Tour at Monticello

Tulips at Monticello bloom like brassy women at a bar, red
lips glistening and full. They remind me of *I
Love Lucy*, throngs of Mrs. Ricardos panicked for spending
Ricky's paycheck on a lime-green dress and violent
fuchsia hat. Eventually, they'll hang their heads
in unison, but for now the giddy yard's enriched

by chaos; my husband and I gawk at the rich
display. They shimmy from their beds like the red
haired beauties of Toulouse-Lautrec, whose plumed heads
flutter like hybrid blooms, their flashing eyes
the oldest trade in town. There's violence
in indulgence. During "Tulipmania," many spent

as much for a rare bulb as one might spend
for a large Dutch house. Craved by poor and rich
alike, for status, beauty, and the scarcity of their violent
hues—two-toned mixes of oxblood, magenta, red—
soon, they were the rage of all Holland, and though I
too am struck by the brazen blooms, slick heads

flushed and plump as vulvas, I can't see losing my head
over a bulb. What do I know? Dutchmen spent
their family fortunes on the trade, and I
guess it's no different than all the other get-rich
quick scams that sucker most of us. I admit I've read
Amway brochures, and envied Pet Rocks their violent

fame, so who can argue against the value of violent
beauty? Except maybe Sultan Ahmed, in 1730 beheaded
for various crimes in Turkey, one of which, readily
recorded by traitors, was his heinous spending
of public money at tulip fairs. Such a price for being rich!
His body conspired against him, his heart and eyes.

There are worse crimes, surely, than loving beauty, though I
sense a pattern—Lucy, Lautrec, Ahmed—in how violent
passions get the best of us. And the fact is, the rich
hues that made those blooms so rare, the frilly heads,
were symptoms of disease. A virus, too, spends
itself on pleasure, settles in the petals, mottled and red.

Who's not a whore for beauty? After the tour we head
home inflamed by the violent horizon, the spent sun
spilling its rich red blood. None of us ever gets enough.

Stirring the Soil

In my mother's house are many pots.
Tureens of fern, anthurium, jade, and planted in the dirt
beside stems lie jagged bits of ancestry, chips of pale blue
cups, yellow plates, the handle off an antique crystal vase.

She stirs the dry soil with the shards, then buries them
like holy fertilizer, vital as the sun and drops of water. They
are the host for lost communicants, these pieces of my mother's
former life; and though they once were fragile, she's learned to
expose their sharpest edge. She lifts a broken saucer to the light,
a white one with minute salmon whorls, then pokes it through
moss and into soil surrounding a bromeliad, its bold mouth
pink with morning song. And I'm drawn to help her tamp
the wedge, nudging cracks veining through the gloss.
And learn from her how beauty blooms with loss.
In my mother's house are many pots.

II

The room within is the great fact about a building.
—Frank Lloyd Wright

High School Cheerleaders at a County Fair

We got lost every year in the House of Mirrors
    where bodies wobbled and
stretched. Once Nicky grinned and said
    that's how it felt screwing Sam B.
in a water bed. We laughed but assumed
    she never had, since we, too, were dizzy
with desire, and after all our Nick
    was just like us: she snapped Bazooka
bubble gum, wore her long hair straight
    behind her ears, her oxfords
well-polished, laced up tight. But days
    were never simple as the black and white
of our shoes. Truth is, Sam laid Nicky
    in his Ford, stripped her letter vest,
checkered skirt, then left her
    months later with a child. Nothing
stayed the same except the fair,
    the pulsing neon strobes
and throbbing songs, that House of Mirrors
    flaunting the grotesque.
Though each flawed face seemed familiar,
    we almost believed it wasn't us
captured in that mutable glass.

Choosing the Right Bride
for Daniel

Check the angle of her wrist when she talks. Is it cocked, palm up,
or fallen like a tulip after frost? Will she be a thrower of darts?

If she walks a dog on a beach, who carries the stick? If she draws
a line in the sand, does she erase it?

She's an antique plate. Would she rather be shattered or gather dust
in a closet? Is she sure? Will she change her mind?

Does she bake does she clean is she kind is she mean will your shirts
be as white as a white picket fence in the right magazine?

Does she add garlic to each dish she cooks? Can she steam rice
without lifting the lid? And gravy—can she make gravy?

Will she starch hand towels for a guest bathroom? Collect tiny soaps
in candy bowls? How many soap operas can she name by heart?

If she finds you reading this guide, will she rip it up, then leave you
in a simple pool of light?—She's the one.

Hoping for the Reconciliation of Friends

They're both incredible people,
    they must be, they married each other,
when once the world spun gently on its axis.

We thought they were perfect together,
    which says more about us than them,
how seductive our own blithe assumptions.

Which revolution tilted them off kilter,
    extinguishing the light from their eyes?
Which revelation tossed them back to earth?

It's a queer math that doesn't quite add up:
    what he gets, what she gets equals so much less
than what they lose. They did their best

to shim the glass house, but every gap filled
    created more. Now they spin their days in separate
spheres, nights circumventing black holes.

Passing each other, sparks fly, and touching
    ignites a huge combustion. We're hopeful still.
Isn't that how the universe was created?

Jane Deals with Infidelity
for JM

She cuts his ties in half,
hangs them over chairs, towel rods,
the door knobs he cocked silently
while she lay watching in the dark
wide awake.

She cuts them to a raw, sharp edge,
they fall from her fists
like tongues, smooth as silk
though she knows they are not.
Like whispers they are beautiful

and false. In each design she finds
a hidden pattern: a checked past
delicately woven that shimmered undetected
for years. A flaw that ran the full length
of him. And so she cuts them up

mid-phrase, drapes them from the couch,
kitchen drawers, window sills that trap
the evening breeze. At times she sees
them move, hears them mouth the same
cool lies:

imperfections, they claim, *are not flaws*;
they add to the beauty of the fabric,
and mixture of texture
is desired. Durability,
they swear, *is not affected.*

Sofa from Goodwill

We spot it under boxes in the back,
   behind rusting racks of books and shoes.
We pull it out—the wooden legs are loose,
   leather cushions slumped like dusty sacks
of grain left in a barn. It's worn
   but comfortable, cheap. I trace small
cracks grown from creases, you run your palm
   across the slick, cool hide, then place it on
my startled inner thigh. This is your way.
   You bargain by a subtle touch of skin,
reminding me that what we need we claim
   in the familiar. It's twenty bucks—we pay,
take it home. Then dust it off, mend
   the legs, and test the ample frame.

When We Least Expect It

one bud opens
        to a blood-red beating
    heart—

                and we're blessed
with outcomes we create
            blindly,

        like silent chromosomes,
those stars that slip through
            dark, fertile pores,

                and entwine.
Now I can't tell my scent apart
        from yours; the tendrils

                of your love lace
with mine, like burst bougainvillea,
        yielding ours.

Practicing Her Breathing

was never how she spent her Friday nights.
    But now she's letting go of all that:
Charlie's Bar, the gold tease of rum, the clumsy
    grope of unfamiliar hands. Instead
she loves the mystery in her womb and
    genuflects just getting out of bed, the heft
of her imbalance reminding her of those misguided
    steps she's taken all her life. She swears
she'll start again, learn to pray, recite
    the golden rule, bill of rights, ten
commandments morning, noon and night,
    she'll even pledge allegiance to the flag,
and finally give up smoking—false haloes
    floating off for good. The rings now
are Borden's two percent, around her mouth,
    eight ounces every meal, then reverently,
as if it were the Host, she tucks a multi-vitamin
    on her tongue, in hopes it negates those crazy days,
the urgent nights, the blur of what she was
    before she recognized what she'd become—
Her rough beast kicks, sucks his thumb.

Whole Notes
for Hannah

I remember swearing once that if by luck
or by some tender stroke I had a daughter,

I'd wipe away the salt from your eyes
and urge you
toward your own whole notes.

Now as you grope my lacteal body,
your tiny hands swiping at my nose, my chin,
the gold around my wrist,

listen to the voices in my breast
as one who hears
the sea inside a shell.

Believe me when I say you are the swell
that breaks upon this world a piercing sound.

After a Flood

I'm counting all the bones about this place,
reciting names I memorized in school—clavicle,
    thorax and sternum, limp veins of loose
electrical wire, intestines of air conditioning tubes,
    and plaster, so much plaster, like dead cells

flaking from walls. The rib-cage of dirty heating
    vents, hides, somewhere, a barely beating heart,
and white tiles, smooth as spinal plates, break
    as if the parched earth reclaimed them—chalked clay
cracking in the sun. But no, it's the heft of water, lifting,

    rising up the table legs, bloating the sofa
like a sponge. I'm wishing I'd listened to my children,
    bought the inflatable beds and dining room set,
plump and slick as tulips newly bloomed. Full sets
    for $28.99   pink and purple chairs filled with air.

We'd seat ourselves and let the water take us, out
    the windows, out the swollen door,
floating through the yard, and down the street,
    waving at our dry, astonished neighbors,
our pruned feet kicking toward the world.

The Surgeon as Patient

The surgeon under a surgeon's knife
feels the slit of each incision
he ever cut. His own body, his life,
throbs with the mock of each decision
to excise when oat bran could suffice.
As morphine liquefies his vision,
he shudders at the gnaw of grating bone.
Sewing's more fun than being sewn.

Post-op and pulsing unaware, the patient
dreams he left his pocked skin, nubbed with cysts,
wadded on the bed and split without consent.
His I.V. bag a purse around his wrist,
he clamored down the hall with such lament
he woke himself, humidifying mist
circling in clouds about his head.
If this is heaven, we're terribly misled.

Discharged, he vows renewed compassion
for arteries hard and thick as trees
and murmuring hearts that skip and ration
beats. Acupuncture might someday succeed
and chicken soup will always be in fashion;
perhaps a surgeon should consider these . . .
But lunching lost in thought with fork and scalpel,
trembling, the surgeon peels his apple.

34

A Mother Considers a Cloned World

It's true we have an eye for imperfection.
My daughter squats, studying the flaws
that burst from her limbs like buds: a stout mole,
a pink ridge of scar, a scab worn proud
as a badge. She loves the constellation of freckles
splayed on her forearm and wrist, and the blue wash
of bruise on her shin. I know her by her knobbed knees

and pout—*she's not too young for artifice, but too young*
to question who she is. She's the one with the in-grown
toenail still caked with yesterday's mud, the one prone
to earaches and hives, and on any given evening,
just before the lightning bugs emerge, you'll find her
in the curve of the old oak, there, where the branch
dips and forks. She's carving her full name in bark.

Does she know how the wind now splits her world?
The queer science tapping at the bone of all
that seems knowable, real? She, too, experiments—
makes mud-pies of dirt, flour, leaves, water enough
to hold it all together. *I wonder can we hold it all together?*
And she's learned to extract the small rocks, to save them
for their own rare concoction, and reconfigure wings

of dead bugs, plump thorax, bulbous-black heads.
She stacks them in an empty Altoid tin. She knows nothing
of the petri dish, brimming with what could be her world,
divided then divided again. *These embryonic cells*
could hold her eyes, her small hands, her own deft
heart. What can she fear of conjuring perfection,
she who loves to switch the limbs of dolls,

or pin the wings of flies onto a raisin?
What can she know of spliced DNA, roiling
in this stew of new ideas, our world both singular
and fertile? Would more of her mean only more

to love? *If she were many, who then would I love?*
She's sleeping now, I stroke her neck, her back, her birthmark
round as a penny—a charm or worry stone, I don't know which.

The Appointed
McQueen's Funeral Home, 1985

Whose job was it to lift your slender arms
      and tug your fingers through the starched sleeves?

Who cupped your head and shifted your shoulders
      to nudge the shirt smooth across your back,

noticing your soft blond curls, the down
      on the nape of your neck, while outside

traffic was stirring, a child threw a ball
      for his dog, once, before skipping to school,

and cafes all over the country prepared
      their ordinary fare, coffee, and eggs

over easy, storefronts propping their doors.
      The world moved on about its business,

none any greater than that of the appointed one
      who gathered you in his arms,

the last one to feel your sweet weight
      as he tucked your white shirt with the finesse

of a florist arranging lilies in a vase.
      How does one account for such luck?

Those Who Chose to Jump
The Twin Towers, 2001

Did you trace
　　your children's names
　　　　in ash imagining

their new class photos
　　the disheveled
　　　　sweet wisps of hair

and did you despite
　　smoky fumes smell again
　　　　the coconut lathered

on your back at the pool
　　your mother in a
　　　　wide-brimmed hat

your sister sporting
　　orange water wings
　　　　and you age four poised

to attempt a perfect dive
　　your body leaning forward
　　　　toes curled around the hot tile

And there reaching out
　　toward all that blue—
　　　　your father's arms

Middle School Social Rules
a found poem

Once you've entered the social,
you may not leave.
There's no spoon dancing,
no shoulder bumping,
no hip grinding against
another student. No kissing,
no hands below the waist,
no conga-line dancing,
or circle dancing,
and no slam dancing
on the dance floor.
No riding on another's
back, no throwing
someone in the air,
no being passed around
by a group, no head
banging, no jumping
around on top of others,
(if you want to jump,
jump straight up and down).
All other school rules apply.

My Son, Age Eight, Makes Tacos

I'm touched by his struggle for precision,
the way he bites his lip in concentration

as he folds the white napkins
till creases sail smoothly into tips.

I want to scoop him up, hug him tight,
tell him the edge is no big deal, nothing in life

is perfect—but I don't. I wince
as he grips the paring knife, chops up lettuce

and tomatoes, small seeds oozing down
the blade. He drops them in their own

glass bowls, along with shredded cheddar
cheese, like separating Legos into piles—red,

yellow, and green. The stove spits a testy
staccato, till finally I hear that metal screech

of spatula on Teflon, prodding meat
and sauce onto a plate. He reaches

for the fragile taco shells spooning each
other snugly in their box, and I cringe as he

pries them apart. I try not to notice
their open mouths as he brings the dish

to the table. Do they sing
an astonished aria—or do they scream?

Stacking Up

You can tell a lot about a person by the way
he loads a dishwasher. Take my husband,
he's compulsive about plates, the way they face,
the way they stand up straight. And utensils—
don't integrate forks and knives. The world,
he thinks, runs smoother if spoons are left
marshalling their own space. Ideally, they shoulder
one another, their little heads peering in sync.
We all know tricks to help our lives stack up—

like pumping gas to hit an even number.
Do you, like me, keep pumping little squirts,
keep pumping just to hit the nearest dime?
And dammit, don't you miss it every time, owing
twenty dollars and one cent? I cringe when I overshoot
that mark as though I'm at some slot machine
in Vegas, till finally the fuel trickles out, blotching
my shoes, my jeans, and that odor, that odor
on my hands, cashes in all the way home.

Sixth Grade Science Fair

I've never considered the effects of radiation
on a Twinkie or whether one can make glue
from milk, but passing through these rows
of oddities—pastries stuck to backboards,
moldy fruit—I'm astonished somebody has.

Here, tacked by their tails is tangible youth; here,
caught in a jar is all the proof we need life is rich.

But what if we could host a different fair,
with light circuits hitched to heaven and hell,
tiny strobes to atomize our sins, and magnets
attracting only good? One to probe our most
unanswerable questions (first place: a scholarship
to bliss): *Why do people suffer? Where is God?*

Hypotheses for these evaporate—conclusions
thicken on our tongues.

And maybe it's all here, what we should know,
like which paper towel absorbs the most,
does a yellow candle burn as fast as green,
purple or red? What's the quickest way to kill
a plant, send electric currents through a lemon?

And you, our son, for whom the world is good,
what grows in light and dust inside your bottle?

In Praise of the Beehive
for Lois Witt and Hazel Talley Evans

Whether you like the style
or not, there's something about
the women. A mystery, an allure.
What hides beneath that piled
minaret, a strange mass crowded
with a nest of creatures never before
identified? A universe in and of itself,
each glistening strand a wealth
of information, a network of charged
electric currents, or highways
(no rest stops or exits) and who,
really, are these women, large-
hearted, elegant, strong dames
with names like *Lois* or *Hazel*
bearing up a world with utmost grace,
an ecosystem whirling in place,
a balanced stratosphere of spiral
coif, though none of us, in fact,
knows what lurks there—
I remember as a child, reaching high
to touch a sprayed turret, wrapped
like the sweetest cotton candy: hair
so soft surely would dissolve, as spun
sugar melting on the tongue.
And how long to forge this odd
creation, to plunder
then restore the pyramid, hurled
upward toward God
like another great wonder
of the world?

Relinquishing the Car Keys for the First Time

Geared up and good to go
with hair gel, baggy jeans,
        our son, sixteen, spins the silver key
on a finger: a planet too hot to hold.
        He's burnin', we know,
for new horizons; sees his path
        like the swath of the Milky Way
kickin' ass with all the big stars,
        while we're still tucking in his tee shirt
and buttoning his jacket, our moony faces
        wan with fear. We call out

remember your seatbelt

but even as we say them
our words vaporize in the night
        like his tail lights fading
in the distance. We recognize we need
        to let go; he's not meant to stay
within our sphere. Hubble's Law
        shows his universe expanding,
which really ought to be a good thing
        if only we could leave it at that.
His deduction—it's harder to take:
        the farther a galaxy

the faster it's shooting away

Practicing the Art of Resistance

She celebrates shoes she didn't buy,
funky shades left glaring from racks, skirts
        that try to wrap themselves around her.
She once dreamt she won a giant sweepstakes,
        and Ed McMahon burst through
her front door as bulbs flashed,
        microphones unfurled. Her prize,
blazoned red upon a check, was a promise
        to remove all her possessions.

She wept in disbelief at her good fortune,
        and pinched herself as piece by piece
she watched the loot depart: the big TV,
        the books, the bloated couch, closets
full of limp, disgruntled clothes, all
        the unframed prints she never hung,
and even the piano, dragged in a drone
        of minor chords. Just she remained,
naked, herself, savoring a gold shaft of light

        that found her, open-armed at last.

Refusing to Set Back the Clock

She knows it's time. Time to wind the hands
back full circle, let an hour loose
upon the earth to forage where it may.

It's true she'd enjoy the extra sleep,
fall back is easy—for once
her hour late is prompt, cool.

But she refuses. Chucks the clock face-down
upon the floor and hides her watch
inside a well-stuffed drawer, with sweaters

she hasn't worn in years. She sees it
as an arbitrary call, suspects
there's some pompous knave of power

playing with our days, our nights,
the hours, while we—good soldiers—click,
salute, obey, resetting well-set lives

in a blink. She fancies technology
has trumped us . . . while minutes tick
beyond our own control, our spirits slip

through outlets we can't touch. Instead
she strokes the sundial in her garden,
as shafts of light quarter up her days.

She'd rather gauge her minutes by this breeze
that drops the swollen hours,
plump, urgent with seed.

III

Any landscape is a condition of the spirit.
—Henri-Frédéric Amiel

Laid Bare

Walking in the woods I found a skin
        discarded by a snake that long since

bellied-by this path. It draped like late day
        sun across my palm. Does the snake

preparing to shed, feel the ease
        of every loosened scale? And has she

any sense of what's gained, as flakes,
        purled and fragile, drop like antique lace

on a rock? The snake has learned to take
        her shedding well, to simply rub her veil

against a stone and muscle through,
        till she becomes mercurial and new,

a thing iridescent, hard to hold—
        more lovely for the grace of letting go.

Again she travels light through tufts of grass,
        the sun lifting shadows from her back.

Gift We Forgot How to Accept

Ophiosaurus ventralis: Eastern glass snake

We saw him as a gift, a glass snake lolling in the yard
like a bike tire abandoned in sun. He smelled us
with a flick of his tongue

and we felt the fullness of luck—the encounter
taut with some meaning we in our daze
couldn't name. He writhed

when we picked him up, so violently he snapped
in half. Stunned, we dropped him in the dirt—
Again he split. Bits of him

reeled toward a hedge, organs bulging like jewels,
and we were left fingers outstretched
staring at loss.

Was it not enough to lie down on grass at a distance,
the ground warming us both? Wouldn't that alone
have been enough?

Each day the sun casts out its consummate net.
See how it returns to the horizon
trawling nothing but light?

Artifacts from Black Lake

Memory is a present that never stops passing.
—Octavio Paz

Remember how Black Lake looked at dusk,
plump frogs, the cypress dripping light,
the fallen logs bearded with moss?

Remember those weekends in the woods,
the six of us, a family, floating in a silver canoe,
our balance even then, tenuous.

But there, lily pads stretched out their palms,
dragonflies tipped their purple wands
and we were safe. Remember how we rooted

sandy roads for arrowheads with serrated
edges, or pieces of notched and fluted flint:
artifacts exalting what had been,

despite their shards? Now gates are rusted,
locked, the farm sold, trailer hauled away. Kudzu
cloaks the cabbage palm, and what we were,

the heft and bulk of us, has scattered
like the hulls of dried seed.
Forgetting finds its own weight to bear—

we feel it, like we once felt together
pinesap stuck warm on the bark,
a mockingbird's ecstatic summer song,

and long gauzy strips of unpaved roads. There,
with paper cups of chipped flint, we held tight
to what was honed, though broken.

Gator on Lake Ashby

A boy grips flowers for his mother,
   wading in a lake's shallow hem,
a dragonfly lighting on his arm.

   For a moment the child doesn't move,
as lace wings brush against his wrist
   a twig baton of iridescent blue.

It's spring, look! a turtle on a log,
   a white bird there across the marsh.
The world, it seems, cannot contain itself—

   lily pads coax with open palms,
urging him *Come, walk on water,*
   his feet, pale fish, gently arching.

He can't see what waits beneath the dark,
   but likes the cool liquid on his skin,
the sun on his forearms and neck.

   When bass jump he sees their silver flash
as coins he reaches up to catch,
   everywhere a richness in the air.

Later, when the parched wind stills,
   and lilies shrivel on their pads,
his mother will recall the loud splash,

   and then the deafening silence—those
seconds when a grip pulled him under—
   and the reeds merely shook their joyful heads.

A Predatory Songbird Without Talons
for NR

*The loggerhead shrike impales victims—mice, small birds, and
insects—on thorns, twigs, or barbed wire before tearing them apart.*
—Audubon

She once loved hearing her father sing,
listening to his voice unfurl
like a bolt of blue silk.
     Now she crouches low,
skitters from the trap of his loose tune,
slips into a whole note,
disappears.

Others see his hands as soft, cool,
each finger like a feather
lifting up a gray wing of a bird.
     Those are not the hands she feels
at night when something stabs her skin,
pins her down, leaves her
twisted and raw.

She remembers a dirt path,
blue sky, a barbed wire fence
around a grassy field,
     then, oozing blood,
a limp, brown mouse dangling like a child's
worn-out sock, the barb, a wire sandspur
through his neck.

First she thought it must be some sick joke
or ritual that pierced the silken throat
and left him, as a sacrificial gift.
     Then she saw the bird, heard the song.
And even now, she feels the notched-beak
pecking, pecking at her
gaped flesh.

On the Suwannee

As children we played along this bank
       where limestone craters the shore.

We balanced on knobs of cypress knees,
       barefoot, baggy jeans rolled up, eager

for a white splash of bass. In one hand
       I gripped a reed and stirred

as you caught minnows in a cup,
       breadcrumbs scattering like ash.

We watched them spiral down and slowly
       sink, then sailed our woven twigs

around the bend. What floats,
       what sinks, what particles dissolve,

I understood those concepts
       better then: the river was clear-black,

rocks were white. But now I find
       what disappears in day

quietly emerges at night, and most
       of the rocks I've kept are really gray.

Floating Dock

The day they lay nude on the dock,
    sun played the river like a riff
        of good jazz, the current

improvising. She wanted to swim with him
    in the dark water, touch his skin
        where tannin turned it gold

below the surface. She wanted his chest
    against hers, the river rising up
        between their breasts,

her hands in the hollow of his back.
    But the river was cold, fast. Instead,
        they spent the day on the dock

rocking gently, assuring themselves
    they'd never drift apart. They didn't notice
        mossed logs, the lily pads silting

around them. Years later, alone, she realized
    she'd leaned too long like the pine,
        turned her cheek like a fern

beside the bank. In fact, she'd misread
    the water: all consonance isn't music.
        Nothing submerged turns gold.

For Days We Watch Your Blood

swishing through an artificial heart
like muddy water rushing

through canyons. How odd
to glimpse this raw and private

journey: to see blood push through
your body, the flooded tributaries

of veins. We swab your lips
with Q-tips dipped in ice.

Years ago they dammed the Colorado
attempting to muzzle that force,

but the body creates its own
hydraulics: a confluence of luck

and will. It arrives in an ordinary cooler,
an Igloo, square, blue and white,

like those we took rafting down
the river. It might have held a six-pack

of Coors, or fresh catch of snapper
yet uncleaned, but instead

it bears your new-found heart,
like a prayer, trembling on ice.

Resisting Pathetic Fallacy

I know it means nothing,

the limp sparrow

fallen by the window
on this, the anniversary
of your death. I study
his open black beak,

broken neck, hyphenated lids,
how wind still shirrs
his downy feathers.

But having known you,
your brazen heart,
what should I think

when a breeze
drops a petal
from a window box
bursting with impatiens—

the red bloom

lighting on his breast?

Fevered Ground

Butterflies keep shifting their range
    seeking a home where heat won't wilt
their mottled wings, and toucans spiral

up foothills to light on ridges
    as yellow saxifrage crawls up the Alps.
The world is fighting a fever; we've lost

the golden toad of Costa Rica, which reminds
    me of that high school frog reeking
of formaldehyde as spellbound we slipped

the knife blade between glazed tendons
    and bone, then slit the belly, guarding
the organs, to study its heart and lungs.

We sketched that crucial loop, so similar to our
    own, noting how blood sent out is called
back home. How careful we were with the dead.

Rhododendron Tunnel

We hike the ridge slowly through red spiked bee balm
and mountain laurel
already bloomed

and amble toward a tunnel: a cat's cradle of desire.
We're drawn to the green waxy leaves,
the white flowers

blushed implosions, and even to the musk of its space.
How coolly this canopy of limbs
embraces

emptiness

*

We enter the long whole note, the held breath, the deep
exhalation: the displacement of being
under wing. Around us,

a filigree of dusk, and scallops of lichen that skirt the trunks
of trees already fallen. So much of what we love
is born of loss.

Emerging in a shudder of light, listen—can you hear it?
the pure sound a bell makes the moment it
first stops

ringing

Pruning

You peel away the ivy twining itself across the plaster
knowing it'll grow back
by June.

There's something sweet about determination
reaching out to claim new terrain
like country roads

spun from college towns we called our own.
There, the gray stone walls,
aging dorms,

the best friends you measured all love by.
What were we but idealists
who saw nothing

in the air and embraced it, like gingko leaves
falling near a square,
each in such radiant

demise. The vine pulls the paint off in patches,
leaving tracks etched
in the past.

It will grow back; it's a temporary fix. You remember
how it hurts to feel
attached.

The Reappearing Boy

When asked the size of our family
I, without thinking, count you.

You, in your best torn jeans,
reappear like a cool magician

performing those ancient tricks—
ears spitting nickels, handkerchiefs

blooming to carnations.
You're the one hidden in the box,

sawn through but bounding out alive,
so radiant the rest of us pale, writhing

like frayed trick ropes,
repairing and repairing ourselves.

Considering the Unreliable Narrator
at Fort DeSoto Beach

I also am other than what I imagine myself to be.
To know this is forgiveness.
—Simone Weil

Even the tide shadows its own retraction lifting
its mirrored hem. The drag of surf

keeps drifting. We've no more genes than a pufferfish
spotted green among kelp, inflating

itself in fear. See how we live with contradictions,
collect them like these

perfect broken shells tossed to shore? The world
is caught in its churning.

Here, tracks of terns disappear like faint marks left
on a lover's neck when sorrow

unbuttoned its blouse. Impermanence like a bird in flight,
circles around us.

Only the sun in blind delirium belts out its one pure note.
I'm toeing a two-step with a ghost crab.

Who's chasing whom as he skitters across the sand
waving his white claws?

Confession to the Muse

Dominance is the dark side of water.
—Matthew Kelty, *Flute Solo*

How quickly we let the world wash over
us, though your womb tries to call us back:
a voice lost across water.

We'll drown in the here, now—waves
mercurial, arresting. The world
is a domineering place.

We've forgotten things we meant to say
and those said dissolve like bits of froth
flung in the white spray

of years. Maybe there's nothing left
to tell—the weight can crush us
in a heartbeat—but I confess

I love this cool force
caught below the dark side of water
where syllables like air effervesce.

Cracks of Light

We grind the last trunk of an old oak
    lost beneath the bricked yard,
its roots buckling up, if not with hope,
    at least a damp persistence. It's hard
killing desire tangled in the musk among
    these shoots. They braced us for years,
who are we to shear them? And how long
    before the stump grinder gnaws
on our own deep want, coarsening
    it to dust? What would we be
without thirst? O let that force
    whetting all the earth spill new seed,
while we, muscling toward cracks
    of light, splinter, but grow back.

How Things Line Up

From any measurable angle you're blessed.
You're certain you don't deserve your luck;

but you, like your dog (your sweet black dog),
have learned to seek the salt in every sweat.

Who cares if life's a bit off-kilter? The sun's
garishly warm, and butterflies daub the sky

blue-flecked, frenzied. Kudzu casts off sobriety,
tugging us beneath its ravenous cape

(one Mississippi—two . . . we disappear . . .).
It's harrowing and beautiful, desire

swallowing us whole. What's left
but the molten core of it, morphing

even our flaws toward what we love?
Like the unset clock on the DVD

that pulsed for years: one night, returning
in the dark, no sound but keys in the lock,

we opened to an unexpected pleasure—
the blinking light, the light itself, meant home.

On the Windowpane

The snail on our kitchen window
                        leaves each night a convoluted trail
        swilled in condensation. I know
                    these hieroglyphics. The detail

  of his erratic path, cul-de-sacs
                        coiling into knots, corkscrews splayed
            across the pane, marks a glistening map
                    of *joie de vivre*, or some would claim

confusion. But witness the will
                of the endeavor! That craving to haul
        the encumbering shell
                        he'll never escape. Maybe all

he needs, all any of us needs, is to get
                    from A to B smoothly with more
        heart. But knowing how hard that is,
                how imperceptible, let's ignore

  the tangled tracks, the riotous sun
                    turning his laps to tears. Why mention
        futility? Haven't we all begun
                inching back to exactly where we began?

Black Dirt

We're more than we can sink our teeth into
    though sometimes just that's
enough. Ours is the pit and the fruit
    and the black dirt deeper than both.

But savoring is the body's state of praise—
    you taught me this. You with your probing
turn of phrase found me waiting at the table.
    Even now, after almost twenty years,

we should toast that sanctifying moment
    when everything dissolves on our tongues
in a wash of brilliant red. Don't think
    we leave too much unsaid,

the whole world's chanting desire:
    the gingko, maidenhair tree,
loses her leaves like a woman lets her hair
    down on a love. Feel the flush

of words. Taste them as the hummingbird
    tastes jewelweed in a brambled field,
so sweet it makes his red throat tremble.
    And the fern, there, beneath the pine,

see how it dances for a touch known only
    as wind? Don't think too much is left
unspoken. Listen. Everywhere
    the world's ripe and hungry.

The Richard Snyder Publication Series

This book is the eleventh in a series honoring the memory of Richard Snyder (1925-1986), poet, fiction writer, playwright and longtime professor of English at Ashland University. Snyder served for fifteen years as English Department chair and was co-founder (in 1969) and co-editor of the Ashland Poetry Press, an adjunct of the university. He was also co-founder of the Creative Writing major at the school, one of the first on the undergraduate level in the country. In selecting the manuscript for this book, the editors kept in mind Snyder's tenacious dedication to craftsmanship and thematic integrity.

Snyder Award Winners:
1997: Wendy Battin for *Little Apocalypse*
1998: David Ray for *Demons in the Diner*
1999: Philip Brady for *Weal*
2000: Jan Lee Ande for *Instructions for Walking on Water*
2001: Corrinne Clegg Hales for *Separate Escapes*
2002: Carol Barrett for *Calling in the Bones*
2003: Vern Rutsala for *The Moment's Equation*
2004: Christine Gelineau for *Remorseless Loyalty*
2005: Benjamin S. Grossberg for *Underwater Lengths in a Single Breath*
2006: Lorna Knowles Blake for *Permanent Address*
2007: Helen Pruitt Wallace for *Shimming the Glass House*